DUCT ★ TAPE PURIM

Jill Colella Bloomfield

KAR-BEN
PUBLISHING

KAR-BEN PUBLISHING®
An imprint of Lerner Publishing Group, Inc.
241 First Avenue North
Minneapolis, MN 55401 USA

Website address: www.karben.com

Main body text set in Bembo Book MT Std regular.
Typeface provided by Monotype Typography.

Library of Congress Cataloging-in-Publication Data

Names: Colella, Jill, author.
Title: Duct tape Purim / by Jill Colella.
Description: Minneapolis : Kar-Ben Publishing , 2022. | Includes bibliographical references and index. | Audience: Ages 7–11 | Audience: Grades 2–3 | Summary: "What do duct tape and Queen Esther have in common? Both are strong, flexible and can withstand very challenging circumstances! Create fun costumes and accessories with duct tape to celebrate the holiday of Purim"— Provided by publisher.
Identifiers: LCCN 2020013929 (print) | LCCN 2020013930 (ebook) | ISBN 9781541534698 (library binding) | ISBN 9781541534773 (paperback) | ISBN 9781728417615 (ebook)
Subjects: LCSH: Tape craft—Juvenile literature. | Duct tape—Juvenile literature. | Purim—Juvenile literature.
Classification: LCC TT869.7 .C65 2021 (print) | LCC TT869.7 (ebook) | DDC 745.5—dc23

LC record available at https://lccn.loc.gov/2020013929
LC ebook record available at https://lccn.loc.gov/2020013930

Manufactured in the United States of America
1-44886-35735-5/11/2022

Contents

CELEBRATE PURIM WITH CREATIVITY

What do duct tape and Queen Esther have in common? Both are strong and flexible, and can withstand very challenging circumstances!

Purim, a holiday that comes in early spring, recalls how brave Queen Esther saved the Jewish people of Persia from wicked Haman's evil plot to destroy them. The story is recounted in the biblical Book of Esther. Families celebrate by wearing costumes, eating three-cornered cookies called hamantaschen, listening to the reading of the Megillah (a scroll containing the story) and making noise with groggers, blotting out the name of the villain Haman. Another way to celebrate the festival is by putting on a Purim spiel, a play that acts out the Megillah. Find inspiration here for creative, crafty duct tape costumes to make your spiel even more fun!

The cloth-like tape was first called duck tape, because it was water repellent like a duck's feathers. Super-strong, but still soft and cloth-like, soldiers used duck tape to fix military vehicles during World War II. The tape was used for other applications, like joining metal air ducts together, and it got its new name: duct tape.

Practical, cheap, and easy to use, crafters began inventing new ways to use duct tape as material for making objects. Duct tape makes it easy to craft cool costumes and accessories, no sewing needed. With a rainbow of colored and patterned duct tape available, grab a roll and get ready to create your very own duct tape Purim gear!

Strong Strings

Did you know that duct tape's extreme strength comes from special fibers woven into a crisscross pattern? Where do you think Esther's strength to be brave came from?

BEFORE YOU GET STARTED

Sticky Supply

Duct tape's super stickiness is great for creating entire outfits without a needle and thread. You won't need zippers or buttons either. Any additional accessories can be purchased at craft stores or found online. You can connect pieces, make straps, and more, just by sticking duct tape strips together. But the amazing stickiness of this tape can also be a challenge. Strips can easily stick together when you don't want them to, making them hard to separate. So work slowly and carefully as you create your costumes. This will help you avoid wasting tape or sticking the wrong pieces together.

Setting Up Your Workspace

It's important to create a clean workspace before beginning your costume crafts. Make sure you have a clear area to work. You don't want your tape to stick to delicate surfaces or pick up bits of trash. Place any tools and supplies in easy reach. And keep track of any small parts in bowls or containers. Be aware that duct tape can be difficult to remove from certain surfaces. It may leave a gummy residue behind. Check with an adult first before placing tape on your work table. Also make sure any items that will be covered in duct tape are okay to use.

Costume Creativity on Purim

Making costumes is all about creativity! A Purim costume can be as wild or wacky as you want. It can have any awesome accessories or gadgets you can imagine. The possibilities are endless! Duct tape is perfect for making anything you dream up easy to create. Stick flat strips together at their edges to make duct tape sheets. Fold long strips into ties or strings. Wad several strips into balls to make sculptural shapes. What other shapes or forms can you create with duct tape? Think about it and try it out! Use your imagination. Then get busy making creative costumes that feature your own unique additions!

Stay Safe

It's important to stay safe when using and wearing duct tape items. Never press duct tape's sticky side directly to skin. Do not place duct tape on your—or someone else's—face. Never place it over eyes, ears, or mouths. And never bind any body part with duct tape. Finally, be careful when using sharp objects, such as scissors. Always check in with an adult before working on the crafts in this book.

KING AHASUERUS'S
CROWN

Craft a crown for the foolish Persian king! More than anything, he liked to throw parties. He demanded that his queen, Vashti, come to a party so he could show off how beautiful she was. When she refused, the king demanded a search for an even more beautiful new wife.

Materials
- measuring tape
- cereal box
- scissors
- ruler
- marker
- duct tape
- optional: gems, craft foam, paint, pipe cleaners

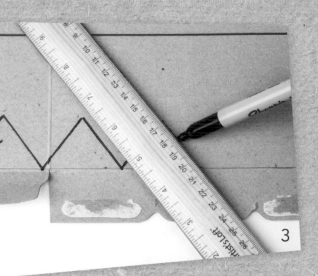

1 Measure around your head with the measuring tape.

2 Take the cereal box apart. Cut the cardboard in half the long way, making two strips. Tape the short edge of one strip to the short edge of the other strip.

3 Use a ruler to draw a flat crown shape onto the cardboard. It should be as long as your head measurement. Cut out the crown.

4 Cover the crown in duct tape. Wrap tape around the sharp points. Cover the back too.

5 Get creative with different shapes, colors, and patterns to decorate the crown. You can even use gems, craft foam, or paint.

6 Tape the crown into a circular shape that fits your head comfortably. Then rule your kingdom in your regal new crown!

Pretend to be King Ahasuerus, and rule Shushan in this regal new crown! Have you ever played Ahasuerus in a Purim spiel?

QUEEN VASHTI'S
ROYAL BRACELETS

Queen Vashti, known for her beauty, would not obey King Ahasuerus's demand, so he sent her away from the palace forever. No Vashti costume is complete without stylish, ornate jewelry!

Materials

- scissors
- cardboard tube
- duct tape

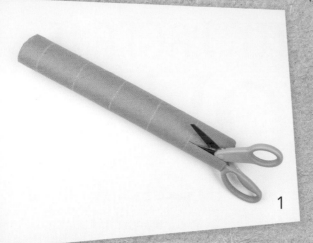

1 Carefully cut a slit along the side of the tube. This will allow the cuffs to be opened over your wrist.

2 Wrap a strip of duct tape around the cardboard tube.

3 Cut along the edge of the strip. Put tape over the edges of the ends. Your cuff is now ready to wear!

4 Repeat Steps 1 through 3, making your way down the tube. Use strips with different patterns to make a variety of fun cuffs!

5 Decorate your cool cuffs in different colors. Wear them together to make a wrist rainbow!

What else can you craft from duct tape for a Vashti costume? Try making a crown fit for a queen.

ESTHER'S BEAUTY PAGEANT
HAIR BOW

A contest was held at the palace to find the most beautiful woman to become Ahasuerus's new queen. Mordechai encouraged his niece, Esther, to enter the pageant, and she did. Ahasuerus could not resist her natural beauty, and he made Esther his queen. Her uncle advised her to keep a secret from the king—that she was Jewish!

Materials
- measuring tape
- duct tape
- scissors
- strong, quick-setting glue
- hair clip, headband, or hair elastic

1 Cut a 16-inch (41 cm) strip of duct tape. Fold it in half the short way, pressing the sticky sides together.

2 Fold each end into the center of the strip. Tape them together. These are the loops of the bow.

3 Cut a 4-inch (10 cm) strip of duct tape. Fold it in half the long way, pressing the sticky sides together.

4 Pinch the center of the bow, puffing the loops out. Tape one end of the strip to the back of the loops. Wrap the strip around the bow once. Tape the end in place on the back.

5 Glue the back of the bow onto a hairclip, headband, or hair elastic. Wear your dazzling duct tape bow anytime!

Esther may have been pretty, but the Talmud suggests that she had more inner beauty— kindness and grace—than the other pageant contestants.

HAMAN'S
HAT

Besides his villainy, his tri-cornered hat may be Haman's most noticeable feature. Create your very own Haman costume topper.

Materials
- measuring tape
- duct tape (silver or black)
- scissors
- stapler

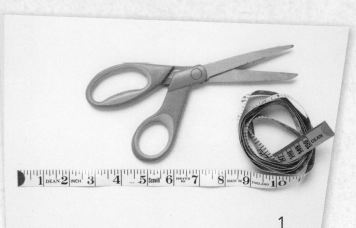

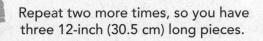
1. Measure around your head with a measuring tape. Cut a strip of duct tape as long as the measurement. Then fold it in half the long way, pressing the sticky sides together. Tape the strip in a loop. This will be the hat's base.

1

2. Cut a strip of duct tape 24 inches (61 cm) long. Fold it in half the short way, pressing the sticky sides together, so you have a piece 12 inches (30.5 cm) long.

3. Repeat two more times, so you have three 12-inch (30.5 cm) long pieces.

4. Use scissors to trim the corners of each strip, so they are slightly rounded.

5. Staple the ends of the three strips together to form a triangle.

2

6. Place the base inside the triangle and staple on each side so hat stays together securely

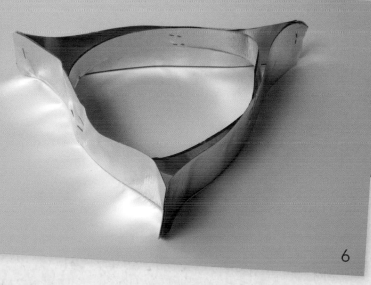
6

QUEEN ESTHER'S RING

Esther won the beauty pageant, but do you think marrying King Ahasuerus was a good prize? Loyal to the Jewish people, Queen Esther used her influence with the king to thwart Haman's plans. Weave a mini duct tape braid to make a vibrant royal ring!

Materials
- measuring tape
- duct tape
- scissors
- binder clip
- cutting board

Measure around your finger with a measuring tape. Add 1 inch (2.5 cm) to the measurement. Cut a strip of duct tape twice as long as the total measurement.

 Fold the strip in half the short way, pressing the sticky sides together. Then cut it into thin, even strips. Cut strips of other colors the same way.

3 Clip the ends of three strips to the top of the cutting board.

4 Braid the strips together. Use small strips of tape to secure the ends of the braid.

5 Wrap the braid around your finger to make sure it fits. Then tape your ring into a loop. Your little tape ring is complete! It slips on and off easily, it's waterproof, and it will never rust!

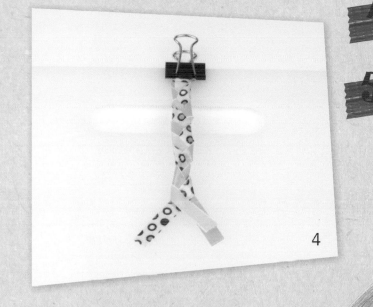

2

4

5

Sticky Tip

To braid, you must work in sets of three. Secure all three strips with a binder clip at the top. Pull one outside strip over the middle strip, making it the new middle strip. Repeat this step with the other outside strip. Keep moving your outside strips to the middle, switching between them as you go. Secure your braid with more tape!

PALACE GUARD'S SHIELD

Want to dress up as a palace guard? Some of them attended King Ahasuerus's giant feast. Ready yourself for a Purim spiel with this sturdy shield.

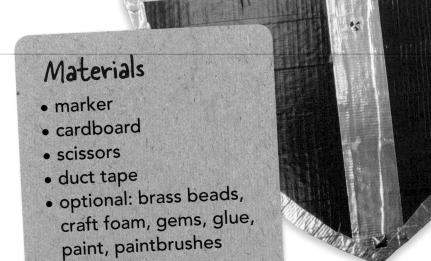

Materials
- marker
- cardboard
- scissors
- duct tape
- optional: brass beads, craft foam, gems, glue, paint, paintbrushes

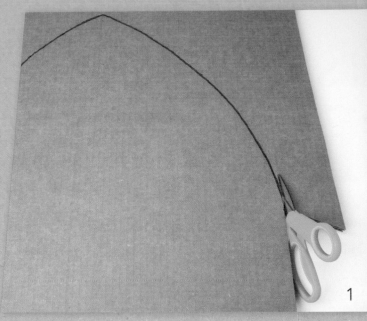

1. Draw a large shield on the cardboard. Cut it out.

2. Cut two strips of duct tape long enough to wrap around your forearm once. Lay one on top of the other, pressing the sticky sides together. Repeat for a second strap. These will be your shield's handles.

3. Tape the handles to the back of the shield. Secure them with extra tape to keep them sturdy.

4. Cover the shield with duct tape. Decorate the shield. Attach brass brads to the front for a shiny, metallic look. Add bright gems, or paint an imaginary crest. Escape sticky situations with your new duct tape shield!

Palace guards Bigthan and Teresh, once plotted to kill the king. Mordechai overheard them and told Esther, who told the king, thwarting their plot. Later in the Purim story, the king remembers that Mordechai had saved his life.

MORDECHAI'S HORSE

Mordechai foils a plot by two palace guards to assassinate Ahasuerus and is honored by the king for this service. Ahasuerus orders Haman to lead Mordechai through the streets on a royal horse to honor him for saving the king's life. Parade like Mordechai! Get your friends together for a Purim parade to show off your duct tape Purim costumes!

Materials
- cardstock paper
- marker
- scissors
- duct tape
- hot glue and hot glue gun
- googly eyes
- broomstick

1 Draw a horse, dragon, or other animal head on the cardstock paper. The drawing should be a side view of the animal's head. Cut it out. Trace it and cut out another one.

2 Cover the cutouts in duct tape. Then cut a strip of cardstock paper as long as their border. Tape the cutouts together, securing the strip in between them. Leave the bottom of the neck open.

3 If your sidekick needs a mane, cut two long strips of duct tape. Lay one strip on top of the other, pressing the sticky sides together. Cut this long strip into shorter thin strips. These will form the mane.

4 Cut two long strips of tape. Lay one strip sticky-side up. Attach the mane strips along one edge. Sandwich these with the other long strip, pressing the sticky sides together. Tape the mane to the head.

5 With an adult's help, hot glue the googly eyes onto your sidekick.

6 Tape the head to the top of a broomstick. Then ride your trusty duct tape sidekick across the land!

SHALACH MANOT
TOTE

The tastiest part of Purim is giving and receiving Purim gift baskets called shalach manot. This fun Purim custom is all about sharing with others and making the day even more festive by giving gifts of food and treats. Tuck some treats into a tote and deliver them to family and friends. Your gift recipients will love the colorful goody bags.

Materials
- duct tape
- scissors
- measuring tape

Cut twenty-eight strips of duct tape 30 inches (76 cm) long. Overlap the long edge of one strip slightly with the long edge of another strip. Keep them sticky-side up. Repeat with the remaining strips until you've formed a rectangle.

2 Fold the rectangle in half the long way, pressing the sticky sides together. Then fold the sheet in half the short way.

3 Cut a strip of tape 36 inches (91 cm) long. Fold it in half the short way, pressing the sticky sides together. Then cut the strip in half the long way. These are your handles!

 Tape the handles to the inside of the bag on either side.

5 Secure the sides of your bag with tape. Fill your bag with goodies for gifting on Purim, or use this sturdy bag for toting books, sports equipment, groceries, craft supplies, and more!

SHUSHAN
ROYAL ROBE

Use an extra-large T-shirt to craft a kingly or queenly costume. Use different colors of duct tape to create a design. Fold a long piece of duct tape in half lengthwise to create a belt to tie around your robe.

Materials
- T-shirt
- duct tape
- scissors
- permanent marker

4

 Select a T-shirt that's a little bit big for you. Lay it flat.

Cut two strips of duct tape long enough to go from the collar of your shirt to the hem.

Cut two strips of tape long enough to go from the edge of one sleeve all the way to the other.

Arrange the strips into an uppercase I shape, sticky sides up. Attach the vertical strip to the horizontal strips.

Remove the shirt. Fill in the I shape with strips of tape, creating a rectangle. Overlap the edge of each strip slightly. Keep the sticky sides facing up.

Create a second rectangle the exact same size. Carefully lay one rectangle on top of the other, pressing the sticky sides together.

5

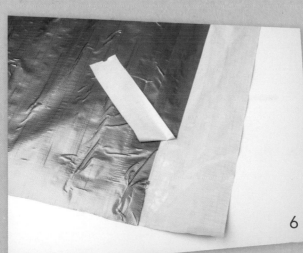

6

Shushan Royal Robe continued on next page

27

7 Repeat steps 2 through 6 to make a matching sheet of tape. This will be the other side of the shirt.

 8 Lay the T-shirt on one of the tape sheets. Trace around it. Cut it out. Repeat this step with the other sheet.

 9 Lay one T-shirt shape on top of the other. Tape along the seams. Leave holes for the sleeves, the collar, and the bottom of the shirt.

 10 Carefully turn the duct tape shirt inside-out. Tape along the seams again.

 11 Decorate your shirt however you want. Mix it up with fun patterns, shapes, and colors. Try making some matching duct tape pants. Then flaunt your terrific tape T-shirt wherever you go!

9

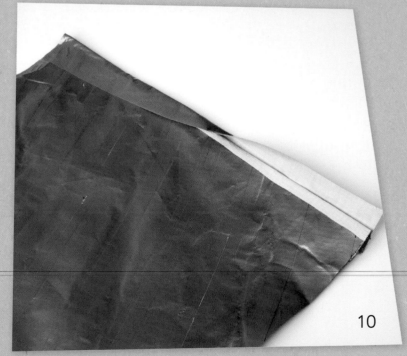

10

STAGE YOUR SPIEL!

Now that you have crafted some clever gear for Purim, it's time to put on a spiel! Mix and match your new creations with clothes from your closet. Get in costume and act out the Megillah, or create your own Purim plays. These Purim spiels can be funny, personalized parodies. Use your favorite stories for inspiration.

Cleanup and Safekeeping

Now that you've turned this tough tape into creative costumes, it's time to clean up. Pick up all tools and supplies. Throw away any ruined strips, or save them for later costumes. Store duct tape rolls out of the sun.

To keep your duct tape costumes in good shape, store them out of the sun or direct heat. If the tape gets too hot, its glue can become gummy. If any of your items become broken from wear, patch and repair them with more tape.

Keep Creating!

Duct tape can be used to make supercool costumes. But the outfits and accessories you create are just the beginning. Get inspired by the duct tape items you make. Think about what additions or additional costumes you could create. Then, gather more tape and keep crafting!

ABOUT PURIM

Purim, a holiday that comes in early spring, recalls how brave Queen Esther saved the Jewish people of Persia from wicked Haman's evil plot to destroy them. The story is recounted in the Biblical book of Esther.

Children and adults celebrate this holiday by wearing costumes, offering charity, and giving gifts of food, called *shalach manot*, to family and friends. An important part of Purim is to hear the reading of the Megillah, a scroll containing the Purim story, and to make noise with groggers, blotting out the name of thc villain Haman. Hamantaschen, pastrics shaped like Haman's three-cornered hat, are a favorite holiday treat. Parades, parties, and carnivals are also fun parts of Purim celebrations.

PHOTO ACKNOWLEDGMENTS
All images Mighty Media. Additional images: monkeybusinessimages/iStockphoto/Getty
Images, p. 7; Lorraine Boogich/iStockphoto/Getty Images, p. 9; Independent Picture Service,
pp. 16-17; Syda Productions/Shutterstock Images, p. 29 (boy). Design elements: mama_mia
/Shutterstock Images; Feng Yu/Shutterstock Images; wongwean/Shutterstock Images;
haya_p/DigitalVision/Getty Images.

Cover: All images Mighty Media. Design elements: haya_p/DigitalVision/Getty Images.